SAINT
NINIAN

BY AELRED, ABBOT OF RIEVAULX

EDITED AND PRESENTED
BY IAIN MACDONALD

FLORIS BOOKS

First published in 1993 by Floris Books

The publisher acknowledges subsidy from the
Scottish Arts Council towards the publication
of this volume.

British Library CIP Data available

ISBN 0-86315-164-7

Printed in Great Britain
by BPCC Wheatons Ltd, Exeter

Contents

Introduction

Tradition tells us that St Ninian was born about the year 360 into a good Cumbrian family. Indeed his father was a chieftain. The Cumbrians, or Cambrians, were a British people. Cumbria at that time stretched from Dumbarton, north of the mouth of the River Clyde to the River Derwent in Cumberland. It stretched eastwards to the Lothians, Berwickshire and Northumberland, thus comprising a large part of Southern Scotland and Northern England. The name Cumbria (or Cambria) is affinitive with Cymru (Wales) for the Cymry (Welsh) are the descendants of those Britons who were later driven westward by the invading Angles.

Just before the time of St Ninian's birth, southern Cambria (Brigantia) was still a well-run Roman province. Hadrian's Wall, built two hundred and fifty years previously, was intact and manned while the Romans maintained fortified camps throughout the Britannic area of Southern Scotland. To the north and west, beyond the abandoned Antonine Wall joining the Firth of Forth to the Firth of Clyde, were the Picts, for the Gaels from Ireland had not yet begun their penetration of Western Scotland.

The young Ninian therefore, as son of a Rex or King within Roman territory would have Roman citizenship and might travel freely throughout the Roman Empire.

In the year 360, however, Scots from Ireland raided Cumbria and at the same time the Picts from the north swept down in a ravaging raid. A mere seven years later, because of the weakness of the Roman garrisons, the Cambrian Britons were exposed to the onslaughts of invading Angles from the east, Scots from Ireland and Picts from the north. Hadrian's Wall was overrun. This was at the time when even Southern England suffered under the attacks of sea-borne invaders from Jutland and the surrounding shores.

In 369 Theodosius repelled the invaders and re-established Roman rule. At the same time he made important changes encouraging the chiefs of the marches to defend their own territory and giving them greater freedom. For the next two decades at least Cumbria was at peace and the Romanization of the culture of the people continued, but at the same time much of the indigenous way of life persisted.

Christianity was rapidly spreading throughout the Roman Empire and even beyond its borders. Many Britons, but not all, were Christian. York already had its bishop and Cumbria came within the orbit of York. Ninian's father was a Christian and so Ninian himself was brought up in a Christian household. Nevertheless older pagan religions still survived in Cumbria. To the north, Christianity had touched the southern Picts, but its hold was tenuous and shifting, while to the east the Angles establishing themselves along the Northumbrian and Berwickshire belt were pure heathen, worshippers of Wotan, Thor and all the Norse gods and goddesses. The Gaels of Ireland followed their druids in their cult, for Christianity had not yet come to Ireland. Such then was the scene while Ninian was a child and youth.

In the present life, Aelred tells us how Ninian, come to manhood, went to Rome (about the year 378). There he was received by the Pope, Damasus I, and studied "the true faith" under such teachers as St Jerome. The next Pope, Siriacus, consecrated Ninian and sent him back to his own people, the Cambrians, to uphold and to further Christianity among them. On his return journey to his native land, Ninian passed through Gaul and came to Tours where he visited and worked with St Martin (383). Thence he travelled northwards until he landed once more in Cambria in about the year 392.

After the calamitous onslaughts of the Picts, Scots and Angles on the northern boundaries of the Roman Empire which, as we have seen, took place before Ninian's departure for Rome, the Romans had re--

established their supremacy in England. Hadrian's Wall had been repaired and freshly garrisoned. In the refashioning of the country, Cambria now formed the principality of Rheged but with the same boundaries as before. Peace had been established with the Picts to the north and east, and the Principality was left unmolested by Angles on the east and Gaels on the west. Thus it was to a peaceful, if religiously confused, region that Ninian came to begin his mission.

Shortly after he began his work, he settled on the Isle of Whithorn on the Solway Coast in Galloway. There he founded his famous abbey, the Candida Casa or White House, so-called because it was (reputedly) the first church in Britain to be built of stone in the continental style, using masons which he had brought with him from Gaul.

From Whithorn, he undertook many journeys throughout Cambria (Rheged), which as we have seen was a very wide region indeed, establishing Christian churches and abbeys as well as preaching Christianity to his fellow-countrymen. Even today legends, place-names and archaeological finds testify to these labours.

Then came his great evangelical mission to the Picts. Although it is not possible to state with accuracy where these travels took him, historians and archaeologists have found traces of his activities along the north-east coast of Scotland through Angus and Aberdeenshire as far north as Cromarty and Easter Ross, It would seem, though, that he did not penetrate to the northern and western Highlands, for the Picts living there were still heathen when two centuries later St Columba undertook his journey to the King of the northern Picts.

In 410 in the face of the Germanic attacks upon the Roman Empire, the Romans withdrew from Britain leaving the Britons to defend themselves against their enemies. How far this withdrawal of the Romans affected Ninian's travels and work, it is not possible to say. Nevertheless Ninian continued his work, based at the Candida Casa until his death in 431, the year in which Saint Patrick began his mission to Ireland.

St Ninian's feast-day is celebrated on September 16.

The Life of St Ninian, presented here, is from the original source written in 1165 by Aelred, Abbot of Rievaulx in Yorkshire, one of the great northern abbeys dissolved during the Reformation.

Aelred himself tells us that he based his Life on an earlier Anglic document. Unfortunately for modern scholarship, Aelred thoroughly despised "the barbarous Anglic language," maintaining the view that such a venerable and saintly life as that of St Ninian could only worthily be told in polished Latin, so that today we have no early Anglo-Saxon or Celtic document relating to the life of St Ninian.

Aelred, or to give him his true Anglian name Aethelred, was born in Hexham, Northumberland about the year 1113. His father, Eilif Lawren, was the priest of the church there (at that time the priests were not enjoined to celibacy). Hexham was then part of Scotland, and Aelred was sent to the court of King David I of Scotland, who following in the footsteps of his saintly mother, Queen Margaret, took great interest in all church matters. It was at that court that Aelred received his education and upbringing. In 1133 he became a Cistercian monk and entered the Abbey of Rievaulx. Ten years later he became Abbot of Rievaulx.

During his life Aelred journeyed throughout Cumbria and Galloway which belonged to the See of York and where traditions and legends concerning St Ninian abounded, and on those travels he collected material for his Life of St Ninian. One other source which Aelred mentions is St Bede. The Venerable Bede (or Beda) (673-735) in his Historia Ecclesiastica Gentis Anglorum *makes a passing reference to St Ninian which Aelred quotes as confirmation of the basic facts.*

Aelred lived and wrote his Life of St Ninian seven hundred years after the saint's death, and beautiful and moving though Aelred's account is, from the historian's point of view there is not much of factual substance. Aelred, like many hagiographers of his period, was writing primarily not as an historian but as a religious seeking to offer this holy life as a good example to others. Indeed many saints' lives of this kind were not much more than a thread on which to hang protracted sermons. Therefore, a great deal remains which we would dearly love to know, and the missing knowledge has to be painstakingly gathered from other sources. Much research, both historical and archaeological, on the life and times of St Ninian has been done in recent years.

The text used here is edited from the nineteenth century translation of Aelred's Latin manuscript by Alexander Penrose Forbes, Bishop of Brechin.

Alexander Forbes edited Aelred's manuscript and published it in Latin with his English translation in his book Historians of Scotland, *Vol. 5. 1874.*

The life of St Ninian

Bishop and confessor, by Aelred, abbot of Rievaulx, translated from the Anglic language into Latin

Prologue

It has been the desire of many of the wise who have lived before us to commit to writing the lives of the saints, especially those who have flourished in their own times. But those with genius and eloquence did this the more usefully as they gratified with polished language the ears of those who listened.

Yet others who, on account of their native barbarism, lacked the faculty of speaking gracefully, nonetheless did not deprive posterity of their own telling of these exemplary lives, albeit in a more simple style. It so happened that a barbarous language obscured the life of the most holy Ninian, and the less it gratified the reader the less it edified him.

Accordingly it pleased your holy affection to impose upon my insignificant self the task of rescuing from a rustic style as if from darkness, and of bringing forth into the clear light of Latin diction, the life of this most renowned man, a life which had been told by those who came before me, truly indeed, but in too barbarous a style.

I undertake therefore the burden which you lay upon me, moved indeed by your prayers but quickened by faith. I will labour, as He will deign to aid me, so to temper my style that on the one hand an offensive roughness does not obscure so elevated a matter, and on the other hand, that a freedom of speech, not so eloquent as fatiguing, does not cheat of the desired fruit of my labour the simplicity of those who cannot appreciate a proper rhetoric. May the grace of the Saviour bless this undertaking.

Preface

Bede's testimony concerning Ninian.

Divine authority recommends to us the glorious life of the most holy Ninian, for the reason that this most blessed one left his own country and his father's house, and learned in a foreign land that which afterwards he taught to his own, being placed by God over the nations and kingdoms, to root out, and to pull down, and to destroy, and to throw down, to build, and to plant. (Jer.1:10)

The Venerable Bede, describing in a very few words the sacred beginnings of the life of this most holy man, the tokens of his sanctity, the dignity of his office, the fruit of his ministry, his most excellent end, and the reward of his toil, writes thus concerning him:

In the year after the incarnation of the Lord 565, at the time when Justin the Less, after Justinian, had received the government of the Roman Empire, there came to Britain out of Ireland a presbyter and abbot, remarkable for his monastic habit and rule, by name Columba, with the intention

of preaching the word of God in the prov-
inces of the Northern Picts; that is, to
those who were separated from the southern regions by lofty and rugged ranges of
mountains. For the southern Picts themselves, who dwell on this side of the same
mountains, had long before abandoned
idolatry, and embraced the faith in the
truth, by the preaching of the word by
Bishop Ninian, a most reverend and holy
man, of the nation of the Britons, who had
at Rome been regularly instructed in the
faith and mysteries of the truth; the seat of
whose episcopate, dedicated to St Martin,
and a remarkable church, where he rests in
the body along with many saints, the nation of the Angles now possesses. That
place, within the province of the Bernicii,
is vulgarly called 'At the White House,' for
that there he built a church of stone in a
way unusual among the Britons. (Bede
Ecclesiastical History, III.iv)

Through the reliable testimony of this great
author, we are acquainted with the origin of St
Ninian, who Bede says was of the race of the
Britons, educated in the rules of the faith in the

Holy Roman Church; as also with his office, as Bede declares him to have been a bishop and preacher of the word of God; and with the fruit of his labours, as Bede shows that, by his toil, the southern Picts were converted from idolatry to the true religion; and with his end, in that he witnesses that Ninian rests along with many saints in the Church of St Martin.

But many things which St Bede seems barely to have touched upon, are detailed at greater length in a book of his Life and Miracles, written in a barbarous style. This book has recorded in historical fashion the way whereby he set out on this path, merited such achievement, and attained to so worthy an end.

Chapter 1

Ninian's birth and education.

The blessed Ninian was born in the island of Britain, of no ignoble family and among a race of the same name which long ago, as they say, took its name from Brutus. It is supposed that Ninian came from that region in the western part of the island where the ocean stretching as an arm, and making as it were on either side two angles, now divides the realms of the Scots and the Angles. This region which until recently belonged to the Angles, is proved not only by historical record but by actual memory of individuals to have had a king of its own.

Ninian's father was a king, by religion a Christian, of such faith in God and of such merit, as to be worthy to have a child who was to provide for what lacked in the faith of his own nation, and by whom another race ignorant of the faith became imbued with the mysteries of our holy religion.

By the guidance of the Holy Spirit, while yet a boy, Ninian shunned whatever was contrary to

religion, chastity, good morals, and against truth.
But whatever was of the law of grace, of good
report, useful to man, or well-pleasing to God, he
ever followed with a mind that was already ma-
ture. Happy was he whose delight was in the law
of the Lord day and night, who like a tree planted
by the waterside brought forth his fruit in due
season (Ps.1:3), seeing that in the vigour of manhood he strenuously fulfilled what he had learned
with the greatest devotion.

He was sparing in food, reticent in speech,
assiduous in study, agreeable in manners, averse
from jesting; and in everything he subjected the
flesh to the spirit. And so bending his mind to the
sacred Scriptures, after he had studied the rules of
the faith from the more learned of his race, the
young man came to see by his own deep insight
and from the inspiration gleaned from the Scriptures, that much was wanting to their perfection.
On this his mind began to be concerned, and not
enduring anything short of perfection, he toiled
and sighed. His heart was hot within him, and at
last in meditation the fire kindled. (Ps.39:4)

"And what," said he, "shall I do? I have sought
in my own land Him whom my soul loves. I
sought Him, but I have not found Him. I will

arise now, and I will compass sea and land. I will seek the truth which my soul loves. (Cant.3:1)

"Surely it needs toil such as this. Was it not said to Peter: *'Thou art Peter, and on this rock I will build my church; and the gates of hell shall not prevail against it'* (Matt.16:18)? Therefore in the faith of Peter there is nothing inferior, nothing obscure, nothing imperfect, nothing against which false doctrine and perverse opinions, like the gates of hell, can prevail. And where is the faith of Peter but in the See of Peter? Thither certainly I must go, that, setting forth from my land, and from my kinsfolk, and from the house of my father, I may be deemed worthy in the land of vision to behold the fair beauty of the Lord, and to visit His temple. (Ps.27:4) The false prosperity of the age smiles on me, the vanity of the world allures me, the love of earthly relationship softens my soul, toil and the weariness of the flesh deter me, but the Lord has said: *He that loves father or mother more than me is unworthy of me, and he that takes not up his cross and follows me is unworthy of me.* (Luke 9:23) I have learned moreover that they who despise the royal court shall attain to the heavenly kingdom."

Therefore, moved by the Holy Spirit, spurning riches, and suppressing all earthly affections, the noble youth set out on pilgrimage, and having crossed the Britannic sea, and entered Italy through the Alps, he arrived safely at the city of Rome.

Chapter 2

He arrives at Rome; he is consecrated bishop by the Pope; his meeting with St Martin; his return to his native land.

The most blessed youth having arrived at Rome, shed tears of devotion before the sacred relics of the Apostles, and with many prayers commended the desire of his heart to their patronage. He then betook himself to the Bishop of the Supreme See; and when he had explained to him the cause of his journey, the Pope accepted his devotion and treated him with the greatest affection as his son. Presently he handed him over to the teachers of truth to be imbued with the disciplines of faith and the sound meanings of Scripture.

But the young man, full of God, took notice that he had not laboured in vain or to no purpose; he learned moreover that in him and his fellow-countrymen many things contrary to sound doctrine had been inculcated by unskilled teachers. Therefore receiving the word of God with the greatest eagerness, like a bee he formed for himself the honeycombs of wisdom by arguments from the different opinions of doctors, as of various kinds of flowers. And hiding them within his heart, he preserved them to be inwardly digested and brought forward for the refreshment of his own soul and for the consolation of many others.

It was a worthy recompense that he who for the love of truth had despised country, wealth, and delights — brought, if I may say so, into the secret chambers of truth and admitted to the very treasures of wisdom and knowledge — should receive in exchange for carnal things spiritual things, for earthly things heavenly things, for temporal blessings eternal goods. Meanwhile, as chaste in body, prudent in mind, provident in counsel, circumspect in every act and word, he was in the mouths of all, it happened that he rose to the favour and friendship of the Supreme Pontiff himself.

After living in a praiseworthy manner for many years in Rome, and having been sufficiently instructed in the sacred Scriptures, he attained to the height of virtue and, sustained on the wings of love, he rose to the contemplation of spiritual things. Then the Roman Pontiff, hearing that some in the western parts of Britain had not yet received the faith of our Saviour, and that some had heard the word of the gospel either from heretics or from men ill instructed in the law of God, moved by the Spirit of God, consecrated Ninian to the episcopate with his own hands, and, after giving him his benediction, sent him forth as an apostle to those people.

There flourished at this time the most blessed Martin, bishop of the city of Tours, whose life rendered glorious by miracles, already described by the most learned and holy Sulpicius, had enlightened the whole world. Therefore Ninian, returning from Rome, full of the Spirit of God, and touched with the desire of seeing him, turned aside to the city of Tours. With what joy and affection he was received by Martin. By the grace of prophetic illumination the worth of the new bishop was not hid from him, whom he recognized as sanctified by the Holy Spirit and sure to be profitable to the salvation of many.

Coming back from exalted things to what is earthly, blessed Ninian asked the saint for the use of masons, saying that he proposed that, as in matters of faith, so in building churches and in creating ecclesiastical offices, he desired to imitate the holy Roman Church. The most blessed Mar-

tin assented to his wishes; and so satiated with
mutual discourse as with heavenly feasts, and with
embraces and tears on both sides, they parted,
holy Martin remaining in his own See, and Ninian hastening on to the work to which the Holy
Spirit had called him.

Upon his return to his own land a great mul-
titude of the people went out to meet him; there
was joy among all, and great devotion, and the
praise of Christ sounded out on all sides, for they
held Ninian for a prophet. Straightaway that
active husbandman of the Lord proceeded to root
up what had been ill planted, to scatter what had
been ill gathered, to cast down what had been ill
built. Having purged the minds of the faithful
from all their errors, he began to lay the foundations of faith; building with the gold of wisdom,
the silver of knowledge, and the stones of good
works: and all the things to be done by the faithful
he taught by word and illustrated by example,
confirming it by many great signs.

Chapter 3

The foundation of the church of Whithorn.
He selected for himself a site in the place which
is now termed Witerna, or Whithorn, which,
situated on the shore of the ocean, and extending
far into the sea on three sides, is accessible only
from the north. There, by Ninian's command, the
masons whom he had brought with him built a
church, which they say was the first in Britain to
be constructed of stone. And having learned that
the most holy Martin, whom he held always in
wondrous affection, had passed from earth to
heaven, he was careful to dedicate the new church
in his honour.

Chapter 4

He heals and converts King Tuduvallus.
Therefore this light began to shine forth in heavenly signs and radiant flames of virtue, and to enlighten darkened minds with the clear and burning word of the Lord, and to warm the cold. There was in that region a king called Tuduvallus (for the whole island lay subject to different kings), whom riches, power, and honour had made proud, and in whom lasciviousness and worldly wealth had so bred haughtiness that he presumed himself to be all-powerful and believed that what anyone else could do was both possible and lawful to him also. He, despising the admonitions of the man of God, secretly depreciated his doctrine and manners, and openly opposed his sound teaching.

But at a certain time, when the king had been more than usually hostile to Ninian, the heavenly Judge suffered no longer that the injury to his servant should go unavenged, but struck him on the head with an unbearable disease, and broke the crown of the head of him that walked in his

sins. To such an extent did his sickness prevail that
a sudden blindness darkened those haughty eyes,
and he who had opposed the light of truth lost
the light of sense; but not in vain, nor to the
increase of his folly. For the poor man lay oppressed by pain, deprived of sight; darkened ex-
ternally, he became enlightened inwardly. When
returning to himself he confessed his sin, seeking
a remedy from him alone to whom he had
hitherto shown himself as an enemy. At last having
called together his relations for counsel, since he
could not go himself, being debarred by his
infirmity, he sent messengers to the man of God,
beseeching him not to enter into judgment with
his servant, nor to reward him according to his
deeds, but to return good for evil, love for hatred.

The most blessed man hearing this, not elated
with human pride, but abounding as ever in the
bowels of compassion, having first offered up
prayer to God, went straightaway to the sick man
with the greatest kindness and devotion. And first
he corrected him with tender reproof, and then
touching the head of the sick man with healing
hand, he signed the blind eyes with the sign of
the saving life. The pain fled, the blindness was
driven away by the coming light, and so it came

to pass that the disease of the body cured the disease of the soul, and the power of the man of God expelled the disease of the body.

Healed therefore both in body and mind, Tuduvallus began thenceforth with all affection to cherish and venerate the saint of God, knowing by experience that the Lord was with him; and directed all his ways, giving him power against everything that exalts itself against the knowledge of Christ, since he was ready to avenge every disobedience and injury inflicted on the servants of Christ.

If, therefore, this contemptuous and proud man, by the grace of humiliation and penance, was deemed worthy to be healed by the holy man, who shall doubt that anyone who with sure faith and sincere and humble heart, seeks the aid of so great a saint for the curing the wounds of inner self, shall obtain a speedy remedy by his holy merits. But let us now go on to other things, which seem all the greater for proving to be contrary to nature itself.

Chapter 5

He clears the presbyter accused of violation.

There was a certain girl in the service of one of the noblemen, fair of face and graceful of aspect, on whom an unchaste young man had cast his eyes and was seized with a blind love. And being unable to subdue the flame of the lust which he had conceived, he began to urge the girl to consent to sin. At length by solicitation or by money, he caused her to conceive sorrow to bring forth iniquity. The unhappy woman yielded to the other's lust, little mindful of the judgment of God, and hoping to evade the eyes of man; but by the swelling of her womb the crime was betrayed, and soon laughter was turned into weeping, pleasure into pain.

But what could she do? whither turn? The law, her parent, her master, were feared. So the unhappy woman made a covenant with death, and put her trust in a lie, believing that she would seem less guilty if she said that she had been deceived or forced by someone of great name. Being urged therefore by the elders to denounce the guilty man, she laid a charge of violence on the presbyter to whom the bishop had delegated the care of the parish.

All were astonished who heard that accusation. They acquitted the girl of the crime which they thought a man of such authority had committed. The good were scandalized, the wicked elated, the common people laughed, and the sacred order was scoffed at; the presbyter, whose fame was injured, was saddened. But the innocence of the priest by the revelation of the Spirit was not hidden from the bishop beloved by God. He bore, however, with impatience the scandal to the Church and the injury to holy religion.

Meanwhile the days of the woman were accomplished and she bore a son, not, as was supposed, to the disgrace of the priest, but to that of the father and the unworthy mother. For the bishop summoned to the Church all the clergy and people, and having exhorted them in a sermon, laid his hands on those who had been baptized. Meanwhile the bold woman, casting aside all shame, bursting in among the people with those who belonged to her, thrust the child in the face of the presbyter, and vociferated in the ears of all the congregation that he was the father

of the child, a violator and deceiver. A clamour
arose among the people; shame among the good,
laughter among the wicked. But the saint, commanding the people to keep quiet, ordered the
new-born child to be brought to him. Then,
inflamed by the Spirit of God, when he had fixed
his eyes on him, he said: "Hear, O child, in the
name of Jesus Christ, say out before this people if
this presbyter begot you."

O marvel! O the strange clemency of God!
Indeed, all things are possible to him that believes;
but what shall I say? The divine power gave
eloquence to the tongue of the infant, and out of
the mouth of a babe and suckling (Ps.8:2), it
confounded the guilty, convicted the liar, ab-
solved the innocent. Accordingly from the infant
body a manly voice was heard; the untaught
tongue formed rational words. Stretching out his
hand, and pointing out his real father among the
people: "This," said he, "is my father. He begot
me. He committed the crime laid upon the priest.
O bishop, thy priest is innocent of this charge."

This was enough. The child thereupon became
silent, to speak again bye and bye according to
the law of nature and the changes of advancing
years. Thanksgiving and praise sounded from the

mouth of all, and all the people exulted with joy, understanding that a great prophet had risen among them, and that God had visited His people. (Luke 1:68)

Chapter 6

Ninian undertakes the conversion of the Picts; he returns home.

Meanwhile the most blessed man, being pained that the devil, driven forth from the earth within the ocean, should find rest in a corner of this island in the hearts of the Picts, girded himself as a strolling wrestler to cast out his tyranny; taking, moreover, the shield of faith, the helmet of salvation, the breastplate of charity, and the sword of the Spirit, which is the word of God. (Eph.6:17).

Fortified by such arms, and surrounded by the society of his holy brethren as by a heavenly host, he invaded the empire of the strong man, with the purpose of rescuing from his power innumerable victims of his captivity: then confronting the southern Picts, in whom persistent error induced them to worship deaf and dumb idols, he taught them the truth of the gospel and the purity of the Christian faith, God working with him, and confirming the word with signs. (Mark 16:20).

The blind see, the lame walk, the lepers are

cleansed, the deaf hear, the dead are raised, those oppressed of the devil are set free. (Luke 7:22).

A door is opened for the Word of God by the grace of the Holy Spirit; the faith is received, error renounced, temples cast down, churches erected. To the font of the saving laver run rich and poor, young and old, young men and maidens, mothers with their children, and, renouncing Satan with all his works, they are joined to the body of the believers by faith, by confession, and by the sacraments. They give thanks to the most merciful God, who had revealed His Name in the islands that are afar off, sending to them a preacher of truth, the lamp of their salvation, calling them His people which were not His people, and them beloved which were not beloved, and them as having found mercy who had not found mercy. (Hos.1:10. Cf. Rom.9:25)

Then the holy bishop began to ordain presbyters, consecrate bishops, distribute the other dignities of the ecclesiastical ranks, and divide the whole land into parishes.

Finally, having confirmed the sons whom he had begotten in Christ in faith and good works, and having set in order all things that referred to the honour of God and the welfare of souls, bidding his brethren farewell, he returned to his own church, where, in great tranquillity of soul, he spent a life perfect in sanctity and glorified by miracles.

Chapter 7

The miracle among the leeks.

It happened one day that Ninian with his brethren entered the refectory to dine, and seeing no pot-herbs or vegetables on the table, he called the brother who had care of the garden, and asked why no leeks or herbs had been placed before the brethren that day.

The brother gardener said: "Father, whatever remained of the leeks and suchlike I planted in the ground only today and the garden has not yet produced anything fit for eating."

Then the saint said: "Go, and whatever your hand finds, gather and bring to me."

Wondering, the brother stood trembling, hesitating what to do; but knowing that Ninian could order nothing in vain, he slowly entered the garden. Then followed a wonder incredible to all save those who know that to him that believes all things are possible. He beheld leeks and other kinds of herbs not only grown, but bearing seed. He was astonished and, as if in a trance, thought that he saw a vision. Finally, returning to himself, and calling to mind the power of the holy man, he gave thanks to God, and culling as much as seemed sufficient, placed it on the table before the bishop. The guests looked at each other, and with heart and voice magnified God working in His saints; and so retired much better refreshed in mind than in body.

Chapter 8

Of the animals and the thieves.

It sometimes pleased the most holy Ninian to visit his flocks and the huts of his shepherds, wishing that the flocks, which he had gathered together for the use of the brethren, the poor and pilgrims, should benefit from the episcopal blessing. Therefore, all the animals being gathered into one place, the servant of the Lord looked upon them, then he lifted up his hand and commended them all to divine protection. Going round them all, and drawing as it were a little circle with the staff on which he leant, he enclosed the cattle, commanding that all within that space should that night remain under the protection of God.

Having done all this, the man of God turned aside to rest for the night at the house of a certain matron. When, after refreshing their bodies with food and their minds with the word of God, all had gone to sleep, a band of thieves appeared and seeing that the cattle were neither enclosed by walls, nor protected by hedges, nor kept in by a ditch, they looked to see if anyone was watching,

or if anything else resisted them. And when they
saw that all was silent, and nothing was present
that might frighten them, they rushed in and
crossed the bounds which the saint had fixed for
the cattle, wishing to carry them all off.

But the divine power that was present resisted
the ungodly who, like brute beasts, minded their
bellies and not their reason; and turned against
them the instrumentality of an irrational animal.
For the bull of the herd rushed upon the men in
fury, and striking at the leader of the thieves,
threw him down and pierced his belly with his
horns, sending forth his life and his entrails together.

Then tearing up the earth with his hoofs, the
bull smote with mighty strength a stone which
happened to be under his foot, and, in a wonder-
ful way, in testimony of the miracle, the foot sunk
into it as if into soft wax, leaving a footmark in
the rock, and by this giving a name to the place.
For to this day the place in the English tongue is
named Farres Last, that is, the Footprint of the
Bull.

Meanwhile, the most blessed father having
finished the solemn service of prayer, went aside,
and finding the man disembowelled and lying

dead among the feet of the cattle, and seeing the others rushing about hither and thither as if possessed by furies, moved with compassion, and turning earnestly to God, besought him to raise the dead. Nor did he cease from tears and entreaties till the same power which had slain him restored the thief not merely to life, but made him safe and sound. For, the power of Christ through the merit of the saint, both smote him and healed him, killed and restored him to life, cast him down to hell and raised him again. (1Sam.2:6-7)

Meanwhile the remaining thieves who, running about the whole night, were contained by a certain madness within the circle which the saint had made, now seeing the servant of God, cast themselves with fear and trembling at his knees imploring pardon. And he, benignly chiding them and impressing upon them the fear of God and the judgment prepared for the rapacious, and giving them his benediction, granted them permission to depart.

Chapter 9

Aelred complains of the morals of his own age; Ninian's way of life; the miracle of the shower.

As I reflect on the devout conversation of this most holy man, I am ashamed of our sloth, and of the laziness of this miserable generation. Which of us, I ask, even among servants, does not more frequently utter jests than things serious, idle things than things useful, carnal things rather than things spiritual, in common conversation and discourse? The mouths that divine grace consecrated for the praise of God and for the celebration of the holy mysteries, are daily polluted by backbiting and secular words, and they weary of the Psalms, the Gospel, and the Prophets. They busy themselves all the day with the vain and base works of man.

Is not the body like the mind, all day in motion while the tongue is idle? Rumours and the doings of wicked men are in men's mouths; religious gravity is relaxed by mirth and idle tales; the affairs of kings, the duties of bishops, the ministries of clerics, the quarrels of princes, above all, the lives and morals of all are discussed. We judge every one but ourselves, and, what is more to be deplored, we bite and devour one another, that we may be consumed one by another. (Gal.5:15)

Not so the most blessed Ninian whose repose no crowd disturbed, whose meditation no journey hindered, whose prayer never grew lukewarm through fatigue. For wherever he went forth, he raised his soul to heavenly things, either by prayer or by contemplation. But as often as, turning aside from his journey, he indulged in rest either for himself or for the beast on which he rode, bringing out a book which he carried about with him for the very purpose, he delighted in reading or singing something, for he felt with the prophet: *O how sweet are thy words unto my throat! yea, sweeter than honey unto my mouth.* (Ps.119:103)

Whence the divine power bestowed such grace upon him, that even when resting in the open air, when reading in the heaviest rain, no moisture ever touched the book on which he was intent. When all around him was everywhere wet with water running upon it, he alone sat with his little book under the waters, as if he were protected by the roof of a house.

Now it happened that the most reverend man

was making a journey with one of his brethren then alive, also a most holy person, by name Plebia, and as his custom was, he solaced the weariness of his journey with the Psalms of David. And when, after a certain distance of the journey they turned aside from the road to rest a little, having opened their Psalters, they proceeded to refresh their souls with sacred reading.

Presently the pleasant calm of the weather becoming obscured by black clouds, there poured down to earth those waters which it had naturally drawn upwards. The light air, like a chamber arching itself around the servants of God, resisted like an impenetrable wall the descending waters. But during the singing, the most blessed Ninian turned off his eyes from the book and, affected somewhat by an unlawful thought, even with some desire, he was thus distracted by a suggestion of the devil. Whereupon at once the shower, invading him and his book, betrayed what was hidden.

Then the brother, who was sitting by him, knowing what had taken place, with gentle re-proof reminded him of his order and age, and showed him how unbecoming such things were in such as he. Straightaway the man of God, coming to himself, blushed that he had been overtaken by a vain thought, and in the same moment drove away the thought and stayed the shower.

Chapter 10

The miracles of Ninian's staff by land and sea.

Meanwhile many, both nobles and men of the middle rank, entrusted their sons to the blessed Pontiff to be trained in sacred learning. He indoctrinated these by his knowledge, he formed them by his example, curbing by a salutary discipline the vices to which their age was prone, and persuasively inculcating the virtues whereby they might live soberly, righteously, and piously.

Once upon a time one of these young men committed a fault which could not escape the saint, and because it was not right that discipline should be withheld, the rods — the severest torments of boys —were made ready. The lad fled in terror, but not being ignorant of the power of the holy man, was careful to carry away with him the staff on which he used to lean, thinking that he had the best comfort for the journey if he took with him something that belonged to the saint.

Fleeing therefore, he sought for a ship to transport him to Scotia. Now it is the custom in that region to fashion out of light branches a kind of

boat in the form of a cup and of such a size that
it can contain three men sitting close together. By
stretching an ox-hide over it, they render it not
only buoyant but actually impenetrable by the
water. Possibly at that time vessels of great size
were built in the same way. The young man
stumbled on one of these lying at the shore, but
not covered with leather, into which, when he
had incautiously entered, I know not whether by
Divine providence or on account of its natural
lightness (for with the slightest touch these vessels
float far out into the waves), straightaway the craft
was carried out to sea.

As the water poured in, the miserable lad stood
in ignorance of what he should do, whither he
should turn, what course he should pursue. If he
abandoned the vessel, his life was in danger;
certain death awaited him if he continued. Then
at last the unhappy boy, repenting his flight,
beheld with pale countenance the waves ready to
avenge the injury he had done. At length, coming
to himself, and thinking that St Ninian was present in his staff, he confessed his fault, as if in his
presence, in a lamentable voice besought pardon,
and prayed for divine aid through his most holy
merits.

Then trusting in the kindness as well as the power of the bishop, the boy stuck the staff in one of the holes. At once the sea trembled and, as if kept back by a divine force, ceased to flow through the open holes. These are Thy works, O Christ, who speaking to Thy disciples, gave to Thy faithful ones this promise: *He that believes in me, the works that I do, he shall do also.* (John 14:12)

For a wind rising from the easterly quarter impelled the vessel gently. The staff, acting as a sail, caught the wind; the staff as helm directed the vessel; the staff as anchor stayed it. The people stood on the western shore, and seeing a little vessel like a bird resting on the waters, neither propelled by sail, nor moved by oar, nor guided by helm, wondered what this miracle might mean.

Meanwhile the young man landed, and that he might make the merits of the man of God more widely known, he planted his staff on the shore, praying God that in testimony of so great a miracle, it might by sending forth roots and receiving sap, produce branches aud leaves and bring forth flowers and fruit.

Divine propitiousness was not wanting to the prayer of the suppliant, and straightaway the dry wood, sending forth roots and covering itself with new bark, put forth leaves and branches and, growing into a considerable tree, made known the power of Ninian to all that beheld it. Miracle was added to miracle. For, to the greater merit of the saint, at the root of the tree a most limpid fountain sprang up, sending forth a crystal stream, winding along with gentle murmur and with lengthened course, delightful to the eye, sweet to the taste, and useful and health-giving to the sick.

Chapter 11

On the death of Ninian; his burial at Whithorn.
The life of the most blessed Ninian, wondrous
with such miracles as these and powerful in the
highest virtues, advanced with prosperous course
to the day of his summons. That day was a day
of exultation and joy to the blessed man, but
of tribulation and misery to the people. He rejoiced, to whom heaven was opened; the people
mourned, who were bereaved of such a father. He
rejoiced, for whom an eternal crown was prepared; they were in sorrow, whose salvation was
endangered. But even his own joy was dashed
with sorrow, since leaving them seemed heavy to
bear, yet to be longer separate from Christ intol-
erable. But Christ, consoling the hesitant soul said:
"Arise, hasten, my friend, my dove, and come.
Arise, my friend," says He, "arise, my dove, arise
through the mind, hasten by desire, come by
love."

Indeed these words well suited the most holy
man, the friend of the Bridegroom, to whom that

heavenly Bridegroom had consigned His bride; to whom He had revealed His secrets; to whom He had opened His treasures. Rightly was that soul termed friend to whom all was love, nothing fear. Christ says, my friend, my dove. O dove, taught indeed to mourn, who, ignorant of the gall of bitterness, used to weep with those that wept, to be weak with the weak, to burn with those that are offended. Arise, hasten, my friend, my dove, and come; for the winter is now past, the rain is over and gone. Then, O blessed man, that winter was indeed past for you, when you were deemed worthy to contemplate the heavenly land which the Sun of righteousness illumines with the light of His glory, which love enkindles, which a wondrous calm, as of springtime, tempers with an unspeakable uniformity of climate. Then for you indeed has passed away that wintry storm which here below hardens the cold hearts of men, in which neither the truth shines nor charity burns; and for you, too, the showers of temptation and the hailstorms of persecution have ceased.

That holy soul, triumphant, has departed into the glory of perpetual freshness. The flowers, says he, appear on the earth. The celestial odour of the

flowers of paradise breathed upon you, O blessed
Ninian, when the company of the martyrs clad
in red, and the confessors clothed in white, smiled
on you as their most familiar friend, and wel-
comed you to their society.

The blessed Ninian, perfect in life and full of
years, passed from this world in happiness and
was carried into heaven, accompanied by the
angelic spirits, to receive an eternal reward, where,
in the company of the apostles, martyrs, holy
confessors and virgins, he fails not to succour
those who hope in him, who cry to him, who
praise him.

He was buried in the Church of Blessed Martin, which he had built from the foundations, and
he was placed in a stone sarcophagus near the
altar, the clergy and people present, with their
voices and hearts sounding forth celestial hymns,
to the accompaniment of sighs and tears.

Here the power which had shone in the living
saint ceases not to make itself manifest about the
body of the departed one, that all the faithful may
acknowledge that he is dwelling in heaven, who
ceases not to work on earth. For at his most sacred
tomb the sick are cured, the lepers are cleansed,
the wicked are terrified, the blind receive their

sight; by all which things the faith of believers is confirmed, to the praise and glory of our Lord Jesus Christ, who lives and reigns with God the Father in the unity of the Holy Ghost, world without end. Amen.

Chapter 12

Miracles of the relics of Ninian

In a deformed poor man

When the most blessed Ninian had been translated into heaven, the faithful people who had loved him in life, frequented with great devotion his most sacred relics; and the Divine Power, approving this reverence and faith, gave evidence by frequent miracles that he whom the common lot had removed from earth was living in heaven.

There was born to one of the people by his own wife a wretched son, the grief of both his parents, the horror of those who beheld him, whom nature had formed contrary to nature, all his members being turned the wrong way. For the joints of his feet being twisted, his heels projected forward, his back adhered to his face, his breast was near the hinder part of his head, with twisted arms his hands rested on his elbows.

What more shall I say? There lay that deformed figure, to whom had been given useless members, a fruitless life, to whom, amid the wreck of his

other members, the tongue alone remained to
bewail his misery, and to move to tears and sorrow
those who beheld and heard him. The sorrow of
his parents was endless. Their grief increased day
by day.

At length the power of the most blessed Ninian, so often experienced, came into their minds,
and, full of faith, they took up that wretched body,
and approaching the relics of the holy man, they
offered the sacrifice of a contrite heart with floods
of tears, and continued in devout prayer till the
hour of vespers.

Then laying that unshapely form before the
tomb of the saint, they said: "Receive, O blessed
Ninian, that which we offer to you, a gift hateful
indeed, but well fitted to prove your power. We,
of a truth, worn out, fatigued, borne down with
sorrow, overcome by weariness, expose it to your
pity. Indeed, if it be a gift, favour is due to those
who offer it; if it be a burden, you are fitter to
bear it, who have more power to lighten it. Here
therefore let him die or live, let him be cured or
let him perish."

Having continued to say these and such things
with tears, they left the sick child before the sacred
relics and went their way. And behold in the

silence of the midnight hour, the poor wretch saw
a man come to him, shining with celestial light,
and glittering in the ornaments of the episcopate,
who, touching his head, told him to arise and be
whole, and give thanks to God his Saviour. And
when he had departed, the wretched being, as if
awaking from a deep sleep, by an easy motion
twisted each member into its natural place, and
having recovered the power of all of them, returned to his home safe and sound. After this he
gave himself wholly up to the church and to
ecclesiastical discipline, and after being first shorn
for the clerical orders, and then ordained presbyter, he ended his life in the service of his father.

In a poor man afflicted with scab
On the fame of the miracle being made known,
many ran together, each one laying his own
trouble before the sacred relics. Among these
there approached a simple man, poor in fortune,
but rich in faith and goodwill, whose whole body
an extraordinary scab had attacked, and so beset
all his members that the skin hardening in mar-
vellous fashion closed the courses of the veins, and
on every side bound up the arteries, so that
nothing but death awaited the patient. The un-

happy man, therefore, approaching the body of
the saint, offered up most devout prayers to altar,
faith, and Lord. His tears flowed, sobs burst forth,
the breast was beaten, the very bowels trembled.
To such faith, to such contrition, neither the
merit of the saint nor the pity of Christ were
lacking, Who therein glorified His saint and mer-
cifully saved the poor man. The poor Adefridus,
for that was his name, did not cease from prayer,
until in a few days he was restored to his former
health.

In a blind girl

There was moreover among the people a certain
girl, Deisuit by name, who was so tormented with
a pain in her eyes that the violence of the disease
took away all power of sight, and darkness creep-
ing around her, even the light of the sun was
hidden from her. It was painful to the patient and
grievous to her sympathizing relations. The skill
of the physicians turned to despair; Ninian, the
only hope that remained, was applied to.

The girl was led by the hand before that most
sacred spot. She was left weeping and wailing;
she asked earnestly; she sought anxiously; she
knocked importunately. The compassionate Jesus

was faithful to His Gospel promise: *Ask, and ye shall receive; seek, and ye shall find; knock, and the door shall be opened unto you.* (Matt.7:7) Therefore to that girl the grace which she sought appeared; the door of pity at which she knocked was opened; the health which she sought was granted; for the darkness was taken away and light was restored. All pain disappeared, and she who had come, led by another to the sacred tomb, returned home guided by her own sight, with great joy of her parents.

In two lepers

There were seen to come into the city two men that were lepers, who deeming it presumptuous to touch with leprosy the holy things, from some distance implored the help of the saint. But coming to the fountain and holding that to be holy whatever Ninian had touched, they thought to be washed there. O new miracle of the prophet Eliseus! O new cleansing, not of one, but of two Naamans! Naaman came in the spirit of presumption, they in that of humility. He came in doubt, they in faith. The king of Syria doubted; the king of Israel doubted; Naaman doubted. The king of Syria, who doubted and was proud, sent his leper to be cleansed, not to the prophet but to the king. The king of Israel doubted, who, on hearing the letter read, rent his clothes, and said, "Am I God, that I can kill and make alive?" Naaman doubted, who, when he heard the advice of the prophet, went away in a rage. Naaman stood in the chariot of pride at the door of Eliseus.

These men in faith and humility cried aloud to the mercy of Ninian. Then that fountain was turned into a Jordan, Ninian into a prophet. The lepers were cleansed by the touch of the laver, and by the merit of Ninian; and their flesh was restored like the flesh of a little child, and they went away healed, to the glory of Ninian, in praise of God, Who works thus marvellously in His saints.

But now this is the end of this book, though not the end of the miracles of St Ninian, which do not cease to shine forth even in our own times to the praise and glory of our Lord Jesus Christ, who with the Father and the Holy Ghost lives and reigns for ever and ever. Amen.

Here ends the Life of St Ninian, bishop and confessor.